DUMP
SODA SECRETS

Publications International, Ltd.

Some of the products listed in this publication may be in limited distribution.

Pictured on the front cover *(clockwise from top left):* Mixed Berry Dump Cake *(page 112),* Pulled Turkey Sandwiches *(page 45),* Mushroom-Barley Soup *(page 5)* and Hot Three-Bean Casserole *(page 96).*

Pictured on the back cover *(left to right):* Coca-Cola® Chili *(page 19),* Cola Float Cupcakes *(page 111)* and Chili Wagon Wheel Casserole *(page 56).*

ISBN: 978-1-68022-237-1

Library of Congress Control Number: 2015949886

Manufactured in China.

8 7 6 5 4 3 2 1

Microwave Cooking: Microwave ovens vary in wattage. Use the cooking times as guidelines and check for doneness before adding more time

The publisher would like to thank The Coca-Cola Company® for the use of their recipes in this publication.

CONTENTS

SOUPS & STARTERS

MUSHROOM-BARLEY SOUP

6 slices bacon, cut into bite-size pieces

1 onion, diced

3 stalks celery, sliced

2 small carrots, peeled and sliced

10 ounces sliced mushrooms

1 teaspoon minced garlic

⅛ teaspoon red pepper flakes

4 cups beef broth

1½ cups water

1 cup uncooked medium barley

½ cup cola

Salt and black pepper

1. Cook bacon in large saucepan over medium-high heat about 10 minutes or until crisp, stirring frequently. Remove bacon to plate; drain all but 1 tablespoon drippings.

2. Add onion, celery, carrots and mushrooms to saucepan; cook about 8 minutes or until vegetables are crisp-tender, stirring occasionally. Add garlic and red pepper flakes; cook and stir 1 minute.

3. Add broth, water, barley, cola, salt and black pepper; bring to a boil. Stir in bacon. Reduce heat to medium-low; cover and simmer 40 minutes or until barley is tender.

Makes 6 servings

 TIP: Before cooking the barley, rinse thoroughly under running water and remove any dirt or debris.

FRENCH LENTIL SOUP

3 tablespoons olive oil

1 medium onion, chopped

1 carrot, chopped

1 stalk celery, chopped

1 clove garlic, minced

8 ounces dried lentils, rinsed and sorted

3 cups chicken broth

1 can (about 14 ounces) stewed tomatoes, undrained

½ cup cola

Salt and black pepper

½ cup grated Parmesan cheese (optional)

1. Heat oil in large saucepan over medium heat. Add onion, carrot, celery and garlic; cook about 8 minutes or until vegetables are tender but not browned, stirring occasionally.

2. Stir in lentils, broth, tomatoes with juice and cola; bring to a boil over high heat. Reduce heat to low; cover and simmer 30 minutes or until lentils are tender. Season with salt and pepper; sprinkle with Parmesan, if desired.

Makes 4 to 6 servings

MAPLE-GLAZED MEATBALLS

2 packages (about 16 ounces each) frozen fully cooked meatballs, partially thawed and separated

1 can (20 ounces) pineapple chunks in juice, drained

1½ cups ketchup

¾ cup maple syrup

⅓ cup 23-flavor cola

¼ cup soy sauce

1 tablespoon quick-cooking tapioca

1 teaspoon dry mustard

½ teaspoon ground allspice

SLOW COOKER DIRECTIONS

1. Combine meatballs, pineapple, ketchup, maple syrup, cola, soy sauce, tapioca, mustard and allspice in slow cooker.

2. Cover; cook on LOW 5 to 6 hours. Stir before serving.

Makes about 48 meatballs

VARIATION: Serve as a main dish over hot cooked rice.

TWIN CHEESE DIP

12 ounces sharp
    Cheddar cheese
1   package (4 ounces)
    Roquefort cheese
1   clove garlic
¾   cup *Coca-Cola®*,
    divided
2   tablespoons soft
    margarine
1   tablespoon grated
    onion
1½ teaspoons
    Worcestershire
    sauce
1   teaspoon dry mustard
¼   teaspoon salt
⅛   teaspoon hot pepper
    sauce

GRATE Cheddar cheese into large mixing bowl. Add crumbled Roquefort. Put garlic through press; add to cheeses with ½ cup *Coca-Cola* and remaining ingredients.

PLACE mixture in food processor; pulse until combined. Gradually add remaining *Coca-Cola*, then process until mixture is fairly smooth, light and fluffy. Pack into covered container. Chill. Best if refrigerated overnight.

Makes about 3 cups

TIP: This dip keeps very well for a week or more. Twin Cheese Dip is good with raw vegetables, as a spread for cocktail breads or crackers or even as a sandwich filling.

ASIAN CHICKEN WINGS

12 chicken wings, tips removed and split at joints *or* 24 chicken drummettes

¼ cup cola

2 tablespoons dry sherry

2 tablespoons soy sauce

2 cloves garlic, minced

Dipping Sauce (optional)

1. Place wings in large resealable food storage bag. Combine cola, sherry, soy sauce and garlic in small bowl; pour over wings. Seal bag; turn to coat. Marinate in refrigerator at least 4 hours or up to 24 hours. Prepare Dipping Sauce, if desired.

2. Preheat broiler. Drain wings; reserve marinade. Place wings on rack of broiler pan; brush with half of reserved marinade.

3. Broil 6 inches from heat 10 minutes. Turn wings; brush with remaining marinade. Broil 10 minutes or until wings are browned and cooked through. Serve with Dipping Sauce, if desired.

Makes 24 appetizers

DIPPING SAUCE: Combine ½ cup mayonnaise, 2 teaspoons soy sauce, 1 teaspoon rice vinegar and ½ teaspoon sesame oil in small bowl. Cover and refrigerate until ready to serve.

SOUTH PACIFIC PORK RIBS

1 to 2 tablespoons
 canola oil, divided

3½ to 4 pounds pork loin
 riblets (about
 20 riblets)

 Salt and black pepper

1 onion, chopped

1 can (20 ounces)
 pineapple chunks
 in juice

¼ cup all-purpose flour

½ cup cola

¼ cup white vinegar

¼ cup ketchup

1 tablespoon packed
 brown sugar

1 tablespoon soy sauce

SLOW COOKER DIRECTIONS

1. Heat 1 tablespoon oil in large skillet over medium-high heat. Season riblets with salt and pepper. Cook in batches, turning to brown all sides and adding additional oil as needed. Transfer to slow cooker. Add onion to skillet; cook and stir 3 to 5 minutes or until softened.

2. Drain pineapple, reserving 1 cup juice. Whisk flour into pineapple juice until well blended. Add cola, vinegar, ketchup, brown sugar and soy sauce to skillet; cook and stir 1 minute. Stir in pineapple juice mixture; cook over medium-low heat until thickened. Pour sauce and pineapple chunks over ribs in slow cooker.

3. Cover; cook on LOW 8 to 10 hours or on HIGH 5 to 6 hours or until tender.

Makes 4 to 6 servings

SPICY BBQ PARTY FRANKS

1 tablespoon butter

1 package (16 ounces) cocktail franks

⅓ cup cola

⅓ cup ketchup

2 tablespoons hot pepper sauce

2 tablespoons packed dark brown sugar

1 tablespoon cider vinegar

1. Melt butter in medium skillet over medium heat. Pierce cocktail franks with fork. Add to skillet; cook until slightly browned.

2. Stir in cola, ketchup, hot pepper sauce, brown sugar and vinegar. Reduce heat to low; cook until sauce is reduced to sticky glaze.

Makes 6 to 8 servings

CAMPFIRE SAUSAGE AND POTATO SOUP

8 ounces kielbasa sausage, cut in half lengthwise, then crosswise into ½-inch slices

1 large baking potato, cut into ½-inch cubes

1 can (about 15 ounces) dark red kidney beans, rinsed and drained

1 can (about 14 ounces) diced tomatoes

1 can (10½ ounces) condensed beef broth

1 medium onion, diced

1 medium green bell pepper, diced

½ cup cola

1 teaspoon dried oregano

1 teaspoon ground cumin

SLOW COOKER DIRECTIONS

1. Combine sausage, potato, beans, tomatoes, broth, onion, bell pepper cola, oregano and cumin in slow cooker.

2. Cover; cook on LOW 8 hours or on HIGH 4 hours.

Makes 6 to 7 servings

BEEF

COCA-COLA® CHILI

1 **pound ground beef**

1 **medium onion, chopped**

4 **stalks celery, chopped**

1 **can (about 15 ounces) tomato sauce**

1 **can (14½ ounces) beef broth**

2 **tablespoons chili powder**

1 **teaspoon garlic powder**

1 **teaspoon paprika**

1 **teaspoon ground cumin**

1 **can (15 ounces) kidney beans, drained**

1 **cup *Coca-Cola*®**

1 **teaspoon hot pepper sauce**

Salt and black pepper

SPRAY 3-quart Dutch oven with nonstick cooking spray. Cook beef, onion and celery over medium-high heat until meat is browned and vegetables are tender. Drain excess fat.

ADD tomato sauce, beef broth, chili powder, garlic powder, paprika and cumin to meat mixture; stir well. Bring to a boil over high heat. Reduce heat and simmer, uncovered, 20 minutes, stirring occasionally.

STIR in beans, *Coca-Cola* and hot pepper sauce. Continue to simmer 10 to 15 minutes. Season to taste with salt and black pepper. Garnish as desired. Serve immediately.

Makes 4 to 6 servings

TIP: Try cooking this chili one day in advance. By cooking the day before, letting it cool and then refrigerating overnight, you give all the flavors in the chili time to blend.

SWEET AND SOUR BRISKET STEW

1 trimmed beef brisket
  (2½ pounds),* cut
  into 1-inch pieces

1 onion, chopped

2 carrots, cut into
  ½-inch slices

1 jar (12 ounces)
  chili sauce

¼ cup cola

2 tablespoons lemon
  juice

1 tablespoon Dijon
  mustard

1 tablespoon packed
  dark brown sugar

1 clove garlic, minced

½ teaspoon salt

¼ teaspoon paprika

¼ teaspoon black
  pepper

3 tablespoons water

1 tablespoon
  all-purpose flour

*Beef brisket has a heavy
layer of fat, which some
supermarkets trim off. If the
meat is trimmed, buy 2½ pounds;
if not, purchase 4 pounds, then
trim and discard excess fat.

SLOW COOKER DIRECTIONS

1. Combine beef, onion, carrots, chili
sauce, cola, lemon juice, mustard,
brown sugar, garlic, salt, paprika
and pepper in slow cooker; mix
well.

2. Cover; cook on LOW 8 hours.

3. *Turn slow cooker to HIGH.* Stir
water into flour in small bowl;
whisk into slow cooker. Cook,
uncovered, 15 minutes or until
thickened.

Makes 6 to 8 servings

COLA SLOPPY JOES

1   pound ground beef
1   onion, finely chopped
¾   cup finely chopped
     green pepper
1½ tablespoons
     all-purpose flour
1   cup cola
½   cup ketchup
2   tablespoons
     white vinegar
1   tablespoon
     Worcestershire
     sauce
2   teaspoons dry
     mustard
½   teaspoon black
     pepper
½   teaspoon salt
     Hamburger buns

1. Brown beef, onion and bell pepper in large saucepan over medium heat, stirring to break up meat. Drain fat. Stir in flour until blended.

2. Add cola, ketchup, vinegar, Worcestershire sauce, mustard, black pepper and salt; cover and simmer 30 minutes, stirring occasionally.

3. Serve on hamburger buns.

Makes 4 to 6 servings

CHILI SPAGHETTI BAKE

1   **pound ground beef**

1   **medium onion, chopped**

1   **can (about 15 ounces) vegetarian chili with beans**

1   **can (about 14 ounces) Italian-style stewed tomatoes, drained**

1½   **cups (6 ounces) shredded sharp Cheddar cheese, divided**

½   **cup sour cream**

¼   **cup cola**

1½   **teaspoons chili powder**

¼   **teaspoon salt**

¼   **teaspoon garlic powder**

⅛   **teaspoon black pepper**

8   **ounces uncooked spaghetti, cooked and drained**

1. Preheat oven to 350°F. Spray 13×9-inch baking dish with nonstick cooking spray.

2. Brown beef and onion in large saucepan over medium heat, stirring to break up meat. Drain fat. Stir in chili, tomatoes, 1 cup cheese, sour cream, cola, chili powder, salt, garlic powder and pepper; mix well.

3. Place spaghetti in prepared baking dish. Add chili mixture; stir until coated. Sprinkle with remaining ½ cup cheese. Cover dish with foil.

4. Bake 30 minutes or until hot and bubbly. Let stand 5 minutes before serving.

Makes 8 servings

BEEF BRISKET

1   center-cut beef
     brisket (3 to
     4 pounds)
1   packet instant onion
     soup mix
2   cans (4 ounces each)
     tomato sauce
     Ground ginger
1   bottle (2 liters)
     Coca-Cola®, divided
12 potatoes
12 carrots

PREHEAT oven to 350°F. Place beef brisket fat-side up in flat roasting pan.

SPRINKLE onion soup mix on top of brisket and pour 2 cans of tomato sauce on top. Sprinkle with ginger. Pour half of 2-liter bottle of *Coca-Cola* over meat.

PLACE whole potatoes and carrots around sides of pan. Add enough water to cover meat.

BAKE 3½ to 4 hours, occasionally spooning sauce over meat. If necessary, add a little more *Coca-Cola* or water to keep meat covered.

MEAT is done when fork-tender. When finished, remove meat from pan and slice fat cap off top. Using electric knife, carefully cut meat across grain into ¼-inch slices and place in casserole dish, covering with sauce. Reserve some sauce to be used as gravy.

Makes 6 servings

TIP: Serve with potatoes, carrots and a fresh loaf of challah (twisted egg bread) for sopping up the gravy.

BBQ SHORT RIBS WITH COLA SAUCE

1 large (17×15 inches) foil bag
  All-purpose flour
1 can (12 ounces) cola
¾ cup honey
1 can (6 ounces) tomato paste
½ cup cider vinegar
1 teaspoon salt
2 cloves garlic, minced
  Dash hot pepper sauce (optional)
4 pounds beef short ribs, cut into 2-inch lengths

1. Preheat oven to 450°F. Place foil bag in 1-inch-deep jelly-roll pan. Spray inside of bag with nonstick cooking spray; dust with flour.

2. Combine cola, honey, tomato paste, vinegar, salt, garlic and hot pepper sauce, if desired, in medium saucepan; bring to a boil over medium-high heat. Reduce heat to medium; cook about 15 minutes or until slightly reduced, stirring occasionally.

3. Dip ribs in sauce to coat; place in single layer in prepared bag. Pour additional 1 cup sauce into bag. Seal bag, leaving headspace for heat circulation by folding open end twice.

4. Bake 1 hour 15 minutes or until ribs are cooked through.

Makes 4 to 6 servings

BARBECUED BEEF SANDWICHES

1 boneless beef chuck shoulder roast (about 3 pounds)

2 cups ketchup

1 medium onion, chopped

⅓ cup cola

¼ cup cider vinegar

2 tablespoons dark molasses

2 tablespoons Worcestershire sauce

2 cloves garlic, minced

½ teaspoon salt

½ teaspoon dry mustard

½ teaspoon black pepper

¼ teaspoon garlic powder

¼ teaspoon red pepper flakes

Sesame seed buns, split

SLOW COOKER DIRECTIONS

1. Cut roast in half; place in slow cooker. Combine ketchup, onion, cola, vinegar, molasses, Worcestershire sauce, garlic, salt, mustard, black pepper, garlic powder and red pepper flakes in large bowl; pour over roast.

2. Cover; cook on LOW 8 to 10 hours or on HIGH 4 to 5 hours.

3. Remove roast to cutting board; cool slightly. Trim excess fat from meat. Shred meat with two forks. Let sauce stand 5 minutes to allow fat to rise. Skim off fat.

4. Return shredded meat to slow cooker; stir to coat with sauce. Adjust seasonings. Cover; cook on HIGH 15 to 30 minutes or until heated through. Serve on buns.

Makes 12 servings

SUPER SIMPLE POT ROAST

1 boneless beef chuck roast (2½ pounds)
1 can (12 ounces) cola
1 bottle (10 ounces) chili sauce
2 cloves garlic, minced

SLOW COOKER DIRECTIONS

1. Combine roast, cola, chili sauce and garlic in slow cooker.

2. Cover; cook on LOW 6 to 8 hours.

Makes 6 servings

CHUNKY BEEF AND PEPPER CASSEROLE

1 pound ground beef

1 cup chopped green bell pepper

1 cup chopped yellow onion

1 can (8 ounces) tomato sauce

¼ cup cola

2 teaspoons Worcestershire sauce

1 clove garlic, minced

½ teaspoon salt

Hot cooked egg noodles

Chopped fresh Italian parsley (optional)

1. Brown beef, bell pepper and onion in large skillet over medium heat, stirring to break up meat. Drain fat.

2. Stir in tomato sauce, cola, Worcestershire sauce, garlic and salt; bring to a boil. Reduce heat to low; cover and simmer 15 minutes.

3. Serve over noodles. Sprinkle with parsley, if desired.

Makes 4 servings

PORK

CHERRY PORK MEDALLIONS

1 tablespoon olive oil

1 pound pork tenderloin, cut into ½-inch-thick medallions

1 jar (10 ounces) cherry preserves

¼ cup cola

2 tablespoons light corn syrup

¼ teaspoon ground cinnamon

¼ teaspoon ground nutmeg

¼ teaspoon ground cloves

¼ teaspoon salt

1. Heat oil in large nonstick skillet over medium heat. Add pork; cook about 2 minutes per side or until browned. Remove pork to plate.

2. Add cherry preserves, cola, corn syrup, cinnamon, nutmeg, cloves and salt to skillet; bring to a boil over medium-high heat, stirring constantly.

3. Return pork to skillet. Reduce heat to low; cover and simmer 8 to 10 minutes or until pork is barely pink in center.

Makes 4 servings

SPICY PORK PO' BOYS

2 tablespoons chili powder

1 tablespoon salt

1 tablespoon onion powder

1 tablespoon granulated garlic

1 tablespoon paprika

1 tablespoon black pepper

1 teaspoon ground red pepper

1 pound boneless pork ribs

½ cup cola

1 tablespoon hot pepper sauce

Dash Worcestershire sauce

½ cup ketchup

4 French rolls, toasted

½ cup prepared coleslaw

1. Combine chili powder, salt, onion powder, garlic, paprika, black pepper and red pepper in small bowl. Rub mixture over pork, coating all sides. Cover and refrigerate at least 3 hours or overnight.

2. Preheat oven to 250°F. Place ribs in Dutch oven. Pour cola, hot pepper sauce and Worcestershire sauce over ribs; stir to coat.

3. Cover and bake about 4 hours or until ribs are fork-tender. Remove ribs to large bowl. Stir ketchup into Dutch oven; cook over medium-high heat 4 to 6 minutes or until sauce has thickened, stirring frequently. Pour sauce over ribs, pulling meat apart with two forks and coating meat with sauce. Serve on rolls with coleslaw.

Makes 4 servings

HAM AND BARBECUED BEAN SKILLET

1 tablespoon vegetable oil

1 cup chopped onion

1 teaspoon minced garlic

1 can (about 15 ounces) kidney beans, rinsed and drained

1 can (about 15 ounces) cannellini or Great Northern beans, rinsed and drained

1 ham steak (½ inch thick, about 12 ounces), trimmed and cut into ½-inch pieces

1 cup chopped green bell pepper

½ cup ketchup

¼ cup cola

¼ cup packed brown sugar

2 tablespoons cider vinegar

2 teaspoons dry mustard

1. Heat oil in large deep skillet over medium-high heat. Add onion and garlic; cook and stir 3 minutes.

2. Add kidney beans, cannellini beans, ham, bell pepper, ketchup, cola, brown sugar, vinegar and mustard; mix well. Reduce heat to low; simmer, uncovered, 10 minutes or until sauce thickens and mixture is heated through, stirring occasionally.

Makes 4 servings

MARINATED PORK TENDERLOIN

1 cup *Coca-Cola*®

¼ cup beef broth

2 tablespoons cider vinegar

1 tablespoon honey mustard

2 small Granny Smith apples, chopped

4 to 6 green onions, finely chopped

2 cloves garlic, minced

1 teaspoon ground cinnamon

½ teaspoon ground ginger

  Salt and black pepper

1 to 1½ pounds whole pork tenderloin

COMBINE *Coca-Cola*, beef broth, vinegar and mustard in large bowl; mix well. Add apples, green onions, garlic, cinnamon, ginger, salt and black pepper to *Coca-Cola* mixture; mix well.

PLACE pork tenderloin in large plastic resealable food storage bag. Pour *Coca-Cola* mixture over pork, turning to coat. Seal bag and marinate in refrigerator at least 3 hours to let flavors blend, turning occasionally.

PREHEAT oven to 350°F. Remove pork from marinade; discard marinade. Place pork in roasting pan. Bake about 25 to 30 minutes or until internal temperature reaches 165°F when tested with meat thermometer inserted into thickest part of pork.

REMOVE pork from oven and transfer to cutting board. Let stand 10 to 15 minutes before carving. Internal temperature will continue to rise 5°F to 10°F during stand time. Serve with applesauce and your favorite side dishes.

Makes 4 to 6 servings

PANAMA PORK STEW

2 small sweet potatoes
   (about 12 ounces),
   peeled and cut into
   2-inch pieces

1 package (10 ounces)
   frozen corn

1 package (9 ounces)
   frozen cut green
   beans

1 cup chopped onion

1¼ pounds pork stew
    meat, cut into
    1-inch cubes

1 can (about 14 ounces)
   diced tomatoes

¼ cup cola

1 to 2 tablespoons
   chili powder

½ teaspoon salt

½ teaspoon ground
   coriander

SLOW COOKER DIRECTIONS

1. Place potatoes, corn, green beans
and onion in slow cooker. Top with
pork. Add tomatoes, cola, chili
powder, salt and coriander.

2. Cover; cook on LOW 7 to 9 hours.

Makes 6 servings

POULTRY

PULLED TURKEY SANDWICHES

1 tablespoon vegetable oil

1 small red onion, chopped

1 stalk celery, trimmed and chopped

3 cups coarsely chopped cooked turkey thigh meat

1 can (8 ounces) tomato sauce

¼ cup ketchup

¼ cup 23-flavor cola or regular cola

1 tablespoon cider vinegar

2 teaspoons Worcestershire sauce

1 teaspoon Dijon mustard

¼ teaspoon chipotle chile powder

⅛ teaspoon salt

4 hamburger buns

1. Heat oil in Dutch oven or large skillet over medium-high heat. Add onion and celery; cook and stir 5 minutes or until tender.

2. Stir in turkey, tomato sauce, ketchup, cola, vinegar, Worcestershire sauce, mustard, chile powder and salt; cover and simmer about 45 minutes or until turkey is fork-tender.

3. Remove turkey from sauce; coarsely shred with two forks. Serve on buns with sauce.

Makes 4 sandwiches

TIP: The turkey filling for these sandwiches freezes well. Try doubling the recipe and freezing leftovers. Thaw the filling in the refrigerator and reheat in the microwave.

COUNTRY CAPTAIN CHICKEN

¼ cup olive oil

4 boneless skinless chicken breast halves

1 medium onion, sliced

1 medium green bell pepper, sliced

1 can (14½ ounces) chicken broth

1 cup *Coca-Cola*®

1 can (14½ ounces) whole tomatoes, undrained and coarsely chopped

1 can (6 ounces) tomato paste

1 teaspoon hot pepper sauce

½ teaspoon ground white pepper

1 bay leaf

2 tablespoons chopped fresh parsley leaves

2 cups hot cooked rice

HEAT oil in large skillet over medium-high heat. Add chicken breasts; cook 3 to 4 minutes on each side or until lightly browned. Remove from skillet; set aside.

ADD onion and bell pepper to skillet. Cook and stir 5 minutes or until vegetables are tender. Add chicken broth and *Coca-Cola* to skillet, scraping up any browned bits from bottom of pan. Add tomatoes, tomato paste, hot pepper sauce, white pepper and bay leaf. Cook and stir 5 minutes or until sauce thickens slightly.

RETURN chicken to skillet and simmer, uncovered, about 15 minutes or until chicken is no longer pink in center.

REMOVE chicken breasts to serving platter. Remove bay leaf from sauce. Pour sauce over chicken and garnish with parsley. Serve over rice.

Makes 4 to 6 servings

COLA-MARINATED SPANISH CHICKEN

1½   pounds bone-in chicken breasts

1¼   cups cola

½   cup pimiento-stuffed green olives, plus additional for garnish

⅓   cup capers, plus additional for garnish

⅓   cup red wine vinegar

2   tablespoons olive oil

2   tablespoons dried oregano

2   cloves garlic, minced

½   teaspoon salt

½   teaspoon black pepper

1½   teaspoons paprika

2   tablespoons chopped fresh parsley

1. Place chicken in large resealable food storage bag. Add cola, ½ cup olives, ⅓ cup capers, vinegar, oil, oregano, garlic, salt and pepper; seal bag and turn to coat. Marinate in refrigerator at least 1 hour or up to 8 hours.

2. Preheat oven to 350°F. Place chicken in 13×9-inch baking dish; pour marinade over chicken. Sprinkle with paprika.

3. Cover and bake 50 minutes to 1 hour or until chicken is cooked through (165°F). Sprinkle with additional olives, capers and parsley.

Makes 4 servings

TIP: Capers are deep green flower buds of a Mediterranean bush that have been preserved in a vinegary brine. Rinse them in cold water to remove excess salt before using.

CASSEROLE BBQ CHICKEN

3 pounds cut-up chicken or chicken breasts, thighs and legs

⅓ cup all-purpose flour

2 teaspoons salt

⅓ cup oil

½ cup onion, finely diced

½ cup celery, finely diced

½ cup green pepper, finely diced

1 cup ketchup

1 cup *Coca-Cola*®*

2 tablespoons Worcestershire sauce

1 tablespoon salt

½ teaspoon hickory smoked salt

½ teaspoon dried basil leaves

½ teaspoon chili powder

⅛ teaspoon black pepper

To reduce foam for accurate measurement, use Coca-Cola® at room temperature and stir rapidly.

RINSE chicken pieces; pat dry. Coat chicken with flour and salt. Brown chicken on all sides in hot oil, then place in 3-quart casserole. Discard drippings.

COMBINE remaining ingredients; mix well. Spoon sauce over chicken, covering all pieces. Cover and bake at 350°F about 1¼ hours or until chicken is fork-tender.

Makes 4 to 6 servings

SIMPLE TURKEY CHILI

1 **pound ground turkey**

1 **small onion, chopped**

1 **can (about 28 ounces) diced tomatoes**

1 **can (about 15 ounces) black beans, rinsed and drained**

1 **can (about 15 ounces) chickpeas, rinsed and drained**

1 **can (about 15 ounces) kidney beans, rinsed and drained**

1 **can (6 ounces) tomato sauce**

⅓ **cup cola**

1 **can (4 ounces) diced green chiles**

1½ **tablespoons chili powder**

1. Cook turkey and onion in large saucepan or Dutch oven over medium-high heat until turkey is no longer pink, stirring to break up meat. Drain fat.

2. Stir in tomatoes, black beans, chickpeas, kidney beans, tomato sauce, cola, chiles and chili powder; bring to a boil. Reduce heat to low; simmer about 20 minutes, stirring occasionally.

Makes 8 servings

SERVING SUGGESTION: Serve chili over split baked potatoes.

HOISIN CHICKEN

½ cup cola

¼ cup soy sauce

2 tablespoons hoisin sauce

2 cloves garlic, minced

1 teaspoon freshly grated ginger

¼ teaspoon red pepper flakes

1½ pounds boneless skinless chicken cutlets

1. Combine cola, soy sauce, hoisin sauce, garlic, ginger and red pepper flakes in medium bowl; mix well.

2. Place chicken in large resealable food storage bag. Pour cola mixture over chicken; seal bag and marinate in refrigerator at least 30 minutes or overnight.

3. Oil grid. Prepare grill for cooking over medium-high heat. Remove chicken from marinade; discard marinade.

4. Grill chicken 2 to 3 minutes per side or until no longer pink in center.

Makes 4 servings

CHILI WAGON WHEEL CASSEROLE

2 teaspoons olive oil

1 pound ground turkey

¾ cup chopped onion

¾ cup chopped green bell pepper

1 can (about 14 ounces) stewed tomatoes, drained

1 can (8 ounces) tomato sauce

¼ cup cola

¾ teaspoon salt

½ teaspoon black pepper

¼ teaspoon ground allspice

8 ounces uncooked wagon wheel or other pasta, cooked and drained

½ cup (2 ounces) shredded Cheddar cheese

1. Preheat oven to 350°F.

2. Heat oil in large ovenproof skillet over medium-high heat. Add turkey; cook and stir 5 minutes or until no longer pink. Add onion and bell pepper; cook and stir until tender.

3. Stir in tomatoes, tomato sauce, cola, salt, black pepper and allspice; cook 10 minutes, stirring occasionally. Add pasta; stir to coat. Sprinkle with cheese.

4. Bake 20 to 25 minutes or until heated through.

Makes 4 to 6 servings

CURRIED CHICKEN AND VEGETABLE STEW

1 tablespoon olive oil

1 pound boneless skinless chicken breasts, cut into ½-inch cubes

1 tablespoon curry powder

3 cups chicken broth

1 can (about 14 ounces) diced tomatoes

2 medium turnips, cut into 1-inch pieces

2 medium carrots, halved lengthwise, then cut crosswise into 1-inch slices

1 medium onion, chopped

½ cup cola

¼ cup tomato paste

½ teaspoon salt

½ cup raisins (optional)

1. Heat oil in large saucepan over medium heat. Add chicken; cook 5 minutes or until lightly browned, stirring occasionally. Add curry powder; cook and stir 1 minute.

2. Stir in broth, tomatoes, turnips, carrots, onion, cola, tomato paste, salt and raisins, if desired; bring to a boil. Reduce heat to low; cover and simmer 15 minutes or until vegetables are tender, stirring occasionally.

Makes 6 servings

SERVING SUGGESTION: Serve with couscous or brown rice.

BLACK BEAN AND TURKEY STEW

3 cans (about 15 ounces each) black beans, rinsed and drained

1½ cups chopped onions

1 cup chicken broth

1 cup sliced celery

1 cup chopped red bell pepper

½ cup cola

4 cloves garlic, minced

1½ teaspoons dried oregano

¾ teaspoon ground coriander

½ teaspoon salt

½ teaspoon ground cumin

¼ teaspoon ground red pepper

6 ounces cooked turkey sausage, thinly sliced

SLOW COOKER DIRECTIONS

1. Combine beans, onions, broth, celery, bell pepper, cola, garlic, oregano, coriander, salt, cumin and red pepper in slow cooker; mix well.

2. Cover; cook on LOW 6 to 8 hours. Stir in sausage. Cover; cook on LOW 10 to 15 minutes.

Makes 6 servings

TIP: For a thicker stew, transfer about 1½ cups bean mixture from the slow cooker to a food processor or blender before adding the sausage; process until smooth. Return the mixture to the slow cooker. (Or use a hand-held immersion blender and blend briefly in the saucepan, leaving the stew chunky.) Proceed with step 2 as directed.

SPICE ISLAND CHICKEN WITH PINEAPPLE RICE

2 tablespoons vegetable oil

1 onion, chopped

2 teaspoons minced fresh garlic

1 teaspoon ground ginger

1 teaspoon five-spice powder

1 can (20 ounces) pineapple chunks in juice, drained

1 can (12 ounces) cola

1 cup ketchup

¼ cup soy sauce

¼ cup packed brown sugar

2 tablespoons white vinegar

4 boneless skinless chicken breasts (about 6 ounces each)

6 cups hot cooked rice

1 can (8 ounces) crushed pineapple, drained

1 tablespoon chopped fresh parsley

1. Preheat oven to 350°F. Spray 13×9-inch baking dish with nonstick cooking spray.

2. Heat oil in medium saucepan over medium heat. Add onion; cook and stir 8 minutes until translucent. Stir in garlic, ginger and five-spice powder; cook and stir 1 minute. Add pineapple chunks, cola, ketchup, soy sauce, brown sugar and vinegar; bring to a boil over medium-high heat. Cook about 15 minutes or until sauce is slightly syrupy. Place chicken in prepared baking dish; pour sauce over chicken.

3. Bake, uncovered, 30 minutes, turning every 10 minutes. If desired, remove chicken to cutting board and cut into 1-inch pieces. (Chicken breasts can also be left whole.)

4. Combine rice, crushed pineapple and parsley; top with chicken and sauce.

Makes 4 servings

OVEN BARBECUE CHICKEN

¾ **cup barbecue sauce**

¼ **cup cola**

2 **tablespoons honey**

2 **tablespoons soy sauce**

2 **teaspoons grated fresh ginger**

½ **teaspoon dry mustard**

1 **whole chicken (about 3½ pounds), cut up**

1. Preheat oven to 350°F. Spray 13×9-inch baking dish or medium roasting pan with nonstick cooking spray.

2. Combine barbecue sauce, cola, honey, soy sauce, ginger and mustard in small bowl; mix well. Place chicken in prepared baking dish; brush with sauce mixture.

3. Bake 45 minutes or until chicken is cooked through (165°F), brushing occasionally with sauce.

Makes 4 to 6 servings

FRANKS AND BEANS

1   can (about 15 ounces) light red kidney or pinto beans, rinsed and drained

4   turkey hot dogs, sliced

1   cup frozen corn

½   cup mild salsa

2   tablespoons cola

2   teaspoons taco seasoning mix

    Chopped fresh cilantro (optional)

    Tortilla chips or corn tortillas, warmed

1. Combine beans, hot dogs, corn, salsa, cola and taco seasoning mix in large skillet; bring to a simmer over medium heat.

2. Cook 5 minutes, stirring occasionally. Garnish with cilantro; serve with tortilla chips.

Makes 4 servings

CHICKEN AND CHILE PEPPER STEW

1 pound boneless skinless chicken thighs, cut into ½-inch pieces

1 pound small potatoes, sliced

2½ cups chicken broth

1 can (about 14 ounces) diced tomatoes

1 cup chopped onion

½ cup cola

2 poblano peppers,* seeded and diced

1 jalapeño pepper,* seeded and finely chopped

2 tablespoons chili powder

3 cloves garlic, minced

1 teaspoon salt

1 teaspoon dried oregano

Poblano and jalapeño peppers can sting and irritate the skin, so wear rubber gloves when handling peppers and do not touch your eyes.

SLOW COOKER DIRECTIONS

1. Combine chicken, potatoes, broth, tomatoes, onion, cola, poblanos, jalapeño, chili powder, garlic, salt and oregano in slow cooker; mix well.

2. Cover; cook on LOW 8 to 9 hours.

Makes 6 servings

TERIYAKI CHICKEN

1 pound skinless boneless chicken breasts, cut into strips

MARINADE

1 cup soy sauce

½ cup *Coca-Cola*®

¼ cup vegetable oil

2 tablespoons orange juice

1 tablespoon minced fresh ginger

1 clove garlic, minced

Salt, pepper and chili powder to taste

COMBINE all marinade ingredients and marinate chicken overnight.

PREHEAT oven to 350°F. Place chicken on well-oiled pan; reserve marinade. Bake about 30 minutes. Remove from oven; slide chicken around in pan to soak up caramelized sauce. Baste with additional marinade and return to oven for another 15 minutes.

Makes 4 to 6 servings

TIP: If you have any chicken left over, simply combine it with mixed greens, sliced bell peppers, green onion and cucumber for a delicious and healthful teriyaki chicken salad.

SEAFOOD

CREOLE SHRIMP

2 tablespoons olive oil

½ cup diced onion

½ cup diced celery

½ cup diced green
    bell pepper

1 teaspoon chili powder

1 can (about 14 ounces)
    diced tomatoes

1 can (8 ounces) tomato
    sauce

½ cup cola

1 tablespoon hot
    pepper sauce

1 tablespoon
    Worcestershire
    sauce

  Salt and black pepper

1½ pounds medium raw
    shrimp, peeled and
    deveined

  Hot cooked rice

2 green onions, sliced

1. Heat oil in Dutch oven over medium-high heat. Add onion, celery and bell pepper; cook and stir until onion is translucent. Stir in chili powder.

2. Add tomatoes, tomato sauce, cola, hot pepper sauce, Worcestershire sauce, salt and black pepper; bring to a boil. Reduce heat to low; simmer, uncovered, about 45 minutes or until thickened, stirring occasionally.

3. Stir in shrimp; simmer 15 minutes. Serve over rice; sprinkle with green onions.

Makes 4 servings

SHRIMP AND SCALLOP FETTUCCINE

1 tablespoon butter

1 small onion, chopped

8 ounces sea scallops

8 ounces medium raw shrimp, peeled and deveined

8 ounces mushrooms, sliced

½ cup water

½ cup cola

1 tablespoon lemon juice

3 tablespoons all-purpose flour

1 teaspoon salt

1 cup half-and-half

1 pound spinach fettuccine, cooked and drained

¼ cup shredded Parmesan cheese (optional)

2 tablespoons chopped fresh parsley (optional)

1. Melt butter in large skillet over medium heat. Add onion; cook and stir until translucent.

2. Stir in scallops, shrimp, mushrooms, water, cola and lemon juice. Reduce heat to medium-low; cover and cook until scallops are opaque and shrimp are pink and opaque, stirring frequently.

3. Blend flour, salt and half-and-half in small bowl. Gradually add to seafood mixture, stirring constantly until thickened.

4. Spoon over fettuccine; sprinkle with Parmesan and parsley, if desired.

Makes 4 to 6 servings

NOTE: There are two types of scallops available: sea scallops and bay scallops. Sea scallops are more widely available and less tender. Bay scallops are smaller, slightly sweeter and more expensive.

SCALLOPS WITH COLA GLAZE

1 tablespoon butter

1¼ pounds sea scallops, rinsed and dried well

2 tablespoons cola

1 tablespoon dry white wine

1 teaspoon soy sauce

1 teaspoon packed brown sugar

1. Heat butter in large skillet over medium-high heat. Add scallops; cook 2 to 3 minutes per side or until scallops are opaque. Remove to plate.

2. Add cola, wine, soy sauce and brown sugar to skillet; cook and stir 20 to 30 seconds or until liquid thickens. Return scallops to skillet; cook just until heated through and coated with glaze. Serve immediately.

Makes 4 servings

BAYOU JAMBALAYA

2 large stalks celery, diced

1 onion, diced

1½ pounds smoked sausage, cut into ¼-inch slices

3 cloves garlic, chopped

1 red bell pepper, diced

1 tablespoon chopped fresh parsley

1 teaspoon dried oregano

1 teaspoon dried thyme

½ teaspoon paprika

1 pound medium raw shrimp, peeled and deveined

3 cups water

1 can (about 14 ounces) diced tomatoes

1½ cups uncooked long grain rice

½ cup dry white wine

½ cup cola

1 bay leaf

1. Combine celery, onion and sausage in large skillet; cook and stir over medium-high heat 5 minutes. Add garlic and bell pepper; cook and stir 3 minutes. Add parsley, oregano, thyme and paprika; cook and stir 1 minute.

2. Add shrimp, water, tomatoes, rice, wine, cola and bay leaf; bring to a boil. Reduce heat to low; cover and simmer 25 minutes or until rice is tender. Remove and discard bay leaf.

Makes 8 servings

TIP: You can make jambalaya with beef, pork, chicken, duck, shrimp, oysters, crayfish, sausage or any combination.

SEAFOOD GRATIN

8 ounces cooked shrimp

8 ounces cooked crabmeat

8 ounces cooked sole, coarsely chopped

8 ounces cooked lobster, coarsely chopped

2 tablespoons butter

2 tablespoons all-purpose flour

½ cup milk

½ cup cola

¾ cup grated Parmesan cheese

Panko bread crumbs

1. Preheat oven to 325°F. Spray six individual gratin dishes or 2-quart shallow baking dish with nonstick cooking spray. Divide shrimp, crabmeat, sole and lobster evenly among prepared gratin dishes.

2. Melt butter in small saucepan over medium heat. Add flour, whisking constantly until mixture is lightly browned. Whisk in milk, cola and Parmesan; cook until mixture is slightly thickened, stirring constantly. Pour over seafood; sprinkle with panko.

3. Bake 20 to 25 minutes or until bubbly and topping is lightly browned. Cool slightly before serving.

Makes 6 servings

COLA PAELLA

2 tablespoons extra virgin olive oil

6 chicken thighs

8 ounces hot Italian sausage, casings removed

1 green bell pepper, cut into strips

1 onion, thinly sliced

1 can (about 14 ounces) stewed tomatoes, undrained

1 can (12 ounces) cola

¾ cup uncooked rice

1 clove garlic, finely chopped

Salt and black pepper

½ cup frozen peas

8 ounces medium raw shrimp, peeled and deveined (with tails on)

1. Heat oil in Dutch oven over medium heat. Brown chicken; remove to plate. Brown sausage, stirring occasionally to break up meat. Drain fat. Return chicken to pan.

2. Add bell pepper and onion; cook and stir until softened. Add tomatoes with juice, cola, rice, garlic, salt and black pepper; bring to a boil over high heat. Reduce heat to low; cover and simmer 20 minutes.

3. Gently stir in peas and shrimp; cook 10 minutes.

Makes 4 to 6 servings

SIDE
DISHES

TART AND TANGY CHERRY SALAD

1 cup sugar-free lemon-lime soda

1 package (4-serving size) sugar-free cherry gelatin

1 can (about 14 ounces) pitted tart red cherries in water

1 can (11 ounces) mandarin orange segments

¼ cup sugar substitute

1 container (8 ounces) thawed frozen whipped topping

¼ cup finely chopped walnuts

1. Pour soda into large microwavable bowl. Microwave on HIGH 1 minute.

2. Whisk in gelatin until completely dissolved. Drain juice from cherries and oranges into gelatin mixture; stir until well blended.

3. Mash cherries with potato masher or fork in medium bowl. Sprinkle sugar substitute over cherries; mix well.

4. Stir cherry mixture, whipped topping and walnuts into gelatin until well blended. Gently fold in oranges. Pour mixture into glass bowl. Refrigerate 2 hours or until firm.

Makes 10 servings

HINT: This recipe can be prepared 1 day in advance. Cover and refrigerate overnight.

ORANGE-SPICED SWEET POTATOES

2 pounds sweet potatoes, peeled and diced

½ cup (1 stick) butter, cut into small pieces

¼ cup packed dark brown sugar

¼ cup cola

Juice of ½ medium orange

1 teaspoon vanilla

1 teaspoon ground cinnamon

½ teaspoon ground nutmeg

½ teaspoon grated orange peel

¼ teaspoon salt

Chopped pecans, toasted* (optional)

To toast pecans, cook in small heavy skillet over medium heat 1 to 2 minutes or until lightly browned, stirring frequently. Immediately remove from skillet; cool before using.

SLOW COOKER DIRECTIONS

1. Combine sweet potatoes, butter, brown sugar, cola, orange juice, vanilla, cinnamon, nutmeg, orange peel and salt in slow cooker; mix well.

2. Cover; cook on LOW 4 hours or on HIGH 2 hours or until sweet potatoes are tender. Sprinkle with pecans, if desired, just before serving.

Makes 6 servings

BOSTON BAKED BEANS

2 cans (about 15 ounces each) navy or Great Northern beans, rinsed and drained

½ cup cola

⅓ cup finely chopped onion

⅓ cup ketchup

2 tablespoons light molasses

2 teaspoons Worcestershire sauce

1 teaspoon dry mustard

½ teaspoon ground ginger

4 slices bacon, cut into 1-inch pieces

1. Preheat oven to 350°F. Combine beans, cola, onion, ketchup, molasses, Worcestershire sauce, mustard and ginger in 11×7-inch baking dish; mix well. Top with bacon pieces in single layer.

2. Bake, uncovered, 40 to 45 minutes or until most liquid is absorbed and bacon is browned.

Makes 4 to 6 servings

BRAISED BEETS WITH CRANBERRIES

2½ pounds beets, peeled and cut into sixths

¾ cup cranberry juice

½ cup dried cranberries

¼ cup cola

2 tablespoons butter, cut into small pieces

2 tablespoons quick-cooking tapioca

1 tablespoon honey

½ teaspoon salt

⅓ cup crumbled blue cheese

Grated orange peel (optional)

SLOW COOKER DIRECTIONS

1. Combine beets, cranberry juice, cranberries, cola, butter, tapioca, honey and salt in slow cooker.

2. Cover; cook on LOW 7 to 8 hours or until beets are tender. Transfer beets to serving bowl; pour half of cooking liquid over beets. Serve warm, room temperature or chilled; sprinkle with blue cheese and orange peel, if desired.

Makes 6 to 8 servings

COLA MASHED SWEET POTATOES

2 large sweet potatoes, peeled, cubed, cooked until tender and drained

¼ cup cola

3 tablespoons butter

¼ teaspoon ground nutmeg

Salt and black pepper

1. Combine sweet potatoes, cola, butter and nutmeg in large bowl; mash with potato masher or fork.

2. Season with salt and pepper.

Makes 4 servings

SWEET-SOUR CABBAGE

1½   **pounds red or green cabbage**

2   **medium apples, unpeeled**

½   **cup *Coca-Cola*®***

2   **tablespoons vinegar**

2   **tablespoons brown sugar**

2   **tablespoons bacon drippings**

1   **teaspoon salt**

½   **to 1 teaspoon caraway seeds**

*To reduce foam for accurate measurement, use Coca-Cola® at room temperature and stir rapidly.

COARSELY shred or cut cabbage (should measure 3 cups).

CORE and dice apples. Combine cabbage, apples and all remaining ingredients in large saucepan.

COVER and simmer until cabbage is tender, about 25 minutes. Stir occasionally.

Makes 4 servings

BBQ BEAN SALAD

⅓ cup spicy barbecue sauce

¼ cup cola

3 tablespoons cider vinegar

1 tablespoon molasses

1 teaspoon hot pepper sauce

½ teaspoon mustard seeds

1 can (about 15 ounces) pinto beans, rinsed and drained

3 plum tomatoes, seeded and coarsely chopped

4 stalks celery, halved lengthwise and sliced

½ cup chopped green onions

Salt and black pepper

1. Combine barbecue sauce, cola, vinegar, molasses, hot pepper sauce and mustard seeds in large bowl; mix well.

2. Add beans, tomatoes, celery and green onions; toss to coat. Season with salt and black pepper.

Makes 4 to 6 servings

TIP: This salad can be stored in the refrigerator for up to 2 days. Bring to room temperature before serving.

COLA CHUTNEY CARROTS

2 cups baby carrots

1 can (12 ounces) cola

1 cup water

3 tablespoons cranberry chutney

1 tablespoon Dijon mustard

2 teaspoons butter

2 tablespoons chopped pecans, toasted*

*To toast pecans, cook in small heavy skillet over medium heat 1 to 2 minutes or until lightly browned, stirring frequently. Immediately remove from skillet; cool before using.

1. Combine carrots, cola and water in medium saucepan; bring to a boil over medium-high heat. Reduce heat to medium-low; simmer about 8 minutes or until carrots are tender.

2. Drain carrots; return to saucepan. Add chutney, mustard and butter; cook and stir until carrots are glazed. Sprinkle with pecans.

Makes 4 servings

NOTE: Mango chutney can be used in place of cranberry chutney.

HOT THREE-BEAN CASSEROLE

2 tablespoons olive oil

1 cup coarsely chopped onion

1 cup chopped celery

2 cloves garlic, minced

1 can (about 15 ounces) chickpeas, rinsed and drained

1 can (about 15 ounces) kidney beans, rinsed and drained

1 cup coarsely chopped tomato

1 can (about 8 ounces) tomato sauce

¾ cup water

¼ cup cola

1 jalapeño pepper,* minced

1 tablespoon chili powder

1½ teaspoons ground cumin

1 teaspoon salt

1 teaspoon dried oregano

¼ teaspoon black pepper

2½ cups (10 ounces) frozen cut green beans

Fresh oregano (optional)

*Jalapeño peppers can sting and irritate the skin, so wear rubber gloves when handling peppers and do not touch your eyes.

1. Heat oil in large skillet over medium heat. Add onion, celery and garlic; cook and stir 5 minutes or until onion is translucent.

2. Add chickpeas, kidney beans, tomato, tomato sauce, water, cola, jalapeño, chili powder, cumin, salt, dried oregano and black pepper; bring to a boil. Reduce heat to low; simmer, uncovered, 20 minutes.

3. Add green beans; simmer 10 minutes or until tender. Garnish with fresh oregano.

Makes 12 servings

SODA
SWEETS

FUDGY COLA BROWNIES

- 4 ounces unsweetened chocolate
- ½ cup (½ stick) butter
- 1 cup granulated sugar
- ¾ cup packed dark brown sugar
- 2 eggs
- 2 tablespoons cola
- 1 cup all-purpose flour
- 1 teaspoon vanilla
  Cola Frosting (recipe follows, optional)

1. Preheat oven to 350°F. Line bottom and sides of 8-inch baking pan with foil; lightly spray foil with nonstick cooking spray.

2. Combine chocolate and butter in large microwavable bowl. Microwave on HIGH 1½ to 2 minutes or until chocolate is melted and mixture is smooth, stirring at 30-second intervals. Stir in granulated sugar and brown sugar until blended. Beat in eggs, one at a time. Stir in cola. Stir in flour and vanilla until blended. Pour batter into prepared pan.

3. Bake 40 to 45 minutes or until toothpick inserted into center comes out clean. Cool completely in pan on wire rack.

4. Prepare Cola Frosting, if desired. Frost brownies.

Makes 12 to 16 servings

COLA FROSTING: Combine ¼ cup (½ stick) butter, 3 tablespoons cola and 2 tablespoons unsweetened cocoa powder in medium saucepan; cook over medium-low heat until butter melts, stirring frequently. Remove from heat; whisk in 1⅓ cups powdered sugar, sifted, and ½ teaspoon vanilla until blended.

COCA-COLA® CHERRY SALAD

1 can cherry pie filling

½ cup water

1 large package cherry gelatin mix

1 can (7½ ounces) crushed pineapple, undrained

1 can (12 ounces) Coca-Cola®

½ cup chopped nuts

1 tub chilled whipped topping

3 ounces cream cheese

BRING pie filling and water to a boil in medium saucepan over high heat. Remove from heat; add gelatin mix. Stir until mixed.

ADD pineapple with juice. Add Coca-Cola; stir to combine.

STIR in nuts; refrigerate until set.

MEANWHILE, mix together whipped topping and cream cheese. Spread or dollop over cooled and set salad.

Makes 8 servings

SCOTTISH OATEN BREAD

2 cups all-purpose flour, plus additional for pan

1 cup old-fashioned oats

½ cup sugar

2½ teaspoons baking powder

1 teaspoon salt

½ teaspoon baking soda

1 egg, beaten

3 tablespoons vegetable oil

½ teaspoon vanilla

1 cup cola

1 cup coarsely chopped dried prunes

½ cup chopped walnuts

1. Preheat oven to 350°F. Generously grease and flour 9×5-inch loaf pan.

2. Combine 2 cups flour, oats, sugar, baking powder, salt and baking soda in large bowl. Add egg, oil and vanilla; stir with fork just until blended. Add cola, prunes and walnuts; mix well. Pour batter into prepared pan.

3. Bake about 1 hour or until toothpick inserted into center comes out clean. Cool in pan on wire rack 20 minutes; remove to wire rack to cool completely. Wrap in foil; store at room temperature overnight before slicing.

Makes 1 loaf

TIP: This moist and fruity quick bread is delicious as is, toasted or spread with cream cheese.

CHILLY CHEER

1 can (16 ounces) whole berry cranberry sauce

1 package (12 ounces) frozen unsweetened raspberries

2 cans (12 ounces each) ginger ale, divided

1. Combine cranberry sauce, raspberries and 1 can ginger ale in blender; blend until smooth.

2. Pour mixture into gallon-size resealable food storage bag. Add remaining 1 can ginger ale; seal bag and shake well. Freeze overnight or until mixture is frozen.

3. To serve, pound bag with meat mallet or side of can until mixture is slushy. Spoon into dessert dishes or wine glasses.

Makes about 10 servings

PINEAPPLE-ORANGE GRANITA

2 cups pineapple-orange juice

¾ cup ginger ale

¼ cup white wine or white grape juice

1. Combine juice, ginger ale and wine in quart-size resealable food storage bag. Seal bag; freeze until firm.

2. Remove from freezer; let stand 15 minutes to soften slightly.

3. To serve, pound bag with meat mallet or side of can until mixture is slushy. Spoon into dessert dishes or wine glasses.

Makes 6 servings

Chilly Cheer

COLA PECAN PIE

1 package (15 ounces) refrigerated pie crusts (2 crusts)

3 eggs

¾ cup sugar

½ cup corn syrup

¼ cup cola

2 tablespoons butter, melted

1½ teaspoons vanilla

¼ teaspoon salt

1½ cups pecan halves

Vanilla ice cream (optional)

1. Preheat oven to 350°F. Press one crust into 9-inch pie plate. Top with remaining crust; gently press crusts together. Fold edges under and flute or crimp edge.

2. Combine eggs, sugar, corn syrup, cola, butter, vanilla and salt in large bowl; mix well. Stir in pecans until well blended. Pour into pie crust.

3. Bake 55 minutes or until set. Serve warm or cold with ice cream, if desired.

Makes 8 to 10 servings

GINGERBREAD DELUXE

1 package (14 ounces) gingerbread mix
1 tablespoon instant coffee
1 tablespoon grated orange peel
¼ cup orange juice
¾ cup *Coca-Cola*®

COMBINE all ingredients. Beat vigorously with spoon until very well blended, about 1½ minutes.

POUR into 8×8×2-inch greased and floured pan. Bake in 350°F oven 30 to 35 minutes or until center springs back when lightly touched.

COOL 10 minutes; remove from pan and set on rack. Serve as hot bread or as dessert with whipped topping.

Makes 4 to 6 servings

CAKES &
CUPCAKES

COLA FLOAT CUPCAKES

1 package (about
   15 ounces) vanilla
   cake mix, plus
   ingredients to
   prepare mix

1 can (12 ounces)
   plus 2 tablespons
   cola, divided

1 container (about
   16 ounces) creamy
   vanilla frosting

   Whipped cream

   Maraschino cherries

1. Preheat oven to 350°F. Line
18 standard (2½-inch) muffin
cups with paper baking cups.

2. Prepare cake mix according to
package directions, using eggs and
oil as directed and substituting
1 can of cola for water. Spoon batter
evenly into prepared muffin cups.

3. Bake according to package
directions for cupcakes. Cool in
pans 5 minutes; remove to wire
racks to cool completely.

4. Beat remaining 2 tablespoons cola
into frosting until well blended.
Frost cupcakes; top with whipped
cream and maraschino cherries.

Makes 18 cupcakes

MIXED BERRY DUMP CAKE

2 packages (12 ounces each) frozen mixed berries, thawed and drained

1 package (about 15 ounces) white cake mix

¼ teaspoon ground cinnamon

1 can (12 ounces) lemon-lime soda

½ cup cinnamon chips

1. Preheat oven to 350°F. Spray 13×9-inch baking pan with nonstick cooking spray.

2. Spread berries in prepared pan. Top with cake mix, spreading evenly. Sprinkle with cinnamon. Slowly pour soda over top, covering cake mix as much as possible. Sprinkle with cinnamon chips.

3. Bake 45 to 50 minutes or until toothpick inserted into center of cake comes out clean. Cool at least 15 minutes before serving.

Makes 12 to 16 servings

ROCKY ROAD CAKE

1 package (about 15 ounces) devil's food cake mix

1⅓ cups cola

3 eggs

½ cup vegetable oil

4 cups mini marshmallows

1 cup chopped walnuts or pecans, toasted*

1 container (16 ounces) hot fudge topping

To toast walnuts, spread on baking sheet. Bake in preheated 350°F oven 5 to 7 minutes or until lightly browned, stirring frequently. Immediately remove from baking sheet; cool before using.

1. Preheat oven to 350°F. Spray 13×9-inch baking pan with nonstick cooking spray.

2. Beat cake mix, cola, eggs and oil in large bowl with electric mixer at low speed 2 minutes or until well blended. Pour batter into prepared pan.

3. Bake 30 minutes or until toothpick inserted into center comes out almost clean. Immediately sprinkle marshmallows over cake; top with walnuts. Cool in pan 15 minutes.

4. Microwave hot fudge topping according to package directions. Drizzle over cake; cool completely.

Makes 12 to 16 servings

CHOCOLATE MYSTERY CAKE

1 package (about 15 ounces) German chocolate cake mix

1½ cups plus 2 tablespoons root beer (not diet soda), divided

2 eggs

¼ cup vegetable oil

1 container (about 16 ounces) vanilla frosting

1. Preheat oven to 350°F. Spray 13×9-inch baking pan with nonstick cooking spray.

2. Beat cake mix, 1½ cups root beer, eggs and oil in large bowl with electric mixer at low speed 30 seconds. Beat at medium speed 2 minutes or until well blended. Spread batter in prepared pan.

3. Bake 30 minutes or until toothpick inserted into center comes out clean. Cool completely in pan on wire rack.

4. Beat remaining 2 tablespoons root beer into frosting until well blended and fluffy. Frost top of cake.

Makes 12 to 16 servings

LEMON-LIME CUPCAKES

1 package (about
    15 ounces)
    lemon cake mix

1¼ cups lemon-lime soda

1 cup vegetable oil

4 eggs

1 teaspoon grated lime
    peel

1 container (8 ounces)
    thawed frozen
    whipped topping

Lime wedges or
    additional grated
    lime peel (optional)

1. Preheat oven to 350°F. Line 24 standard (2½-inch) muffin cups with paper baking cups.

2. Beat cake mix, soda, oil, eggs and lime peel in large bowl with electric mixer at medium speed 2 minutes or until well blended. Spoon batter evenly into prepared muffin cups.

3. Bake 20 minutes or until toothpick inserted into centers comes out clean. Cool in pans 10 minutes; remove to wire racks to cool completely.

4. Top cupcakes with whipped topping; garnish with lime wedges. Serve immediately.

Makes 24 cupcakes

ISLAND DELIGHT DUMP CAKE

3 ripe mangoes, peeled and cubed (about 4½ cups)

1 package (about 15 ounces) pineapple cake mix

1 can (12 ounces) lemon-lime or orange soda

½ cup chopped macadamia nuts (optional)

1. Preheat oven to 350°F. Spray 13×9-inch baking pan with nonstick cooking spray.

2. Spread mangoes in prepared pan. Top with cake mix, spreading evenly. Slowly pour soda over top, covering cake mix as much as possible. Sprinkle with macadamia nuts, if desired.

3. Bake 35 to 40 minutes or until toothpick inserted into center of cake comes out clean. Cool at least 15 minutes before serving.

Makes 12 to 16 servings

CHOCOLATE CHERRY COLA CUPCAKES

1 jar (8 ounces)
   maraschino cherries
   in syrup
1 package (about
   15 ounces) dark
   chocolate cake mix,
   plus ingredients to
   prepare mix
1 can (12 ounces) cola
1 can (21 ounces) cherry
   pie filling, drained
1 container (about
   16 ounces) whipped
   cream cheese or
   vanilla frosting

1. Preheat oven to 350°F. Line 24 standard (2½-inch) muffin cups with paper baking cups.

2. Drain maraschino cherries, reserving syrup. Set aside 2 tablespoons syrup for frosting. Prepare cake mix according to package directions, using eggs and oil as directed and substituting cola for water. Stir in remaining maraschino cherry syrup and cherry pie filling until blended. Spoon batter evenly into prepared muffin cups.

3. Bake according to package directions for cupcakes. Cool in pans 5 minutes; remove to wire racks to cool completely.

4. Beat reserved 2 tablespoons marachino cherry syrup into frosting until well blended. Frost cupcakes; top with cherries.

Makes 24 cupcakes

DECADENT CHOCOLATE DELIGHT

- 1 package (about 15 ounces) chocolate cake mix
- 1 package (4-serving size) chocolate instant pudding and pie filling mix
- 1 cup cola
- 1 cup (8 ounces) sour cream
- 4 eggs
- 1 cup semisweet chocolate chips
- ¾ cup vegetable oil
- Vanilla ice cream

SLOW COOKER DIRECTIONS

1. Spray slow cooker with nonstick cooking spray.

2. Combine cake mix, pudding mix, cola, sour cream, eggs, chocolate chips and oil in large bowl; mix well. Pour batter into slow cooker.

3. Cover; cook on LOW 3 to 4 hours or on HIGH 1½ to 1¾ hours. Serve warm with ice cream.

Makes 12 servings

METRIC CONVERSION CHART

VOLUME MEASUREMENTS (dry)

1/8 teaspoon = 0.5 mL
1/4 teaspoon = 1 mL
1/2 teaspoon = 2 mL
3/4 teaspoon = 4 mL
1 teaspoon = 5 mL
1 tablespoon = 15 mL
2 tablespoons = 30 mL
1/4 cup = 60 mL
1/3 cup = 75 mL
1/2 cup = 125 mL
2/3 cup = 150 mL
3/4 cup = 175 mL
1 cup = 250 mL
2 cups = 1 pint = 500 mL
3 cups = 750 mL
4 cups = 1 quart = 1 L

VOLUME MEASUREMENTS (fluid)

1 fluid ounce (2 tablespoons) = 30 mL
4 fluid ounces (1/2 cup) = 125 mL
8 fluid ounces (1 cup) = 250 mL
12 fluid ounces (1 1/2 cups) = 375 mL
16 fluid ounces (2 cups) = 500 mL

WEIGHTS (mass)

1/2 ounce = 15 g
1 ounce = 30 g
3 ounces = 90 g
4 ounces = 120 g
8 ounces = 225 g
10 ounces = 285 g
12 ounces = 360 g
16 ounces = 1 pound = 450 g

DIMENSIONS

1/16 inch = 2 mm
1/8 inch = 3 mm
1/4 inch = 6 mm
1/2 inch = 1.5 cm
3/4 inch = 2 cm
1 inch = 2.5 cm

OVEN TEMPERATURES

250°F = 120°C
275°F = 140°C
300°F = 150°C
325°F = 160°C
350°F = 180°C
375°F = 190°C
400°F = 200°C
425°F = 220°C
450°F = 230°C

BAKING PAN SIZES

Utensil	Size in Inches/Quarts	Metric Volume	Size in Centimeters
Baking or	8×8×2	2 L	20×20×5
Cake Pan	9×9×2	2.5 L	23×23×5
(square or	12×8×2	3 L	30×20×5
rectangular)	13×9×2	3.5 L	33×23×5
Loaf Pan	8×4×3	1.5 L	20×10×7
	9×5×3	2 L	23×13×7
Round Layer	8×1 1/2	1.2 L	20×4
Cake Pan	9×1 1/2	1.5 L	23×4
Pie Plate	8×1 1/4	750 mL	20×3
	9×1 1/4	1 L	23×3
Baking Dish	1 quart	1 L	—
or Casserole	1 1/2 quart	1.5 L	—
	2 quart	2 L	—